The 7 Laws Of Motivation:

Explode Your Motivation And Create A Mindset Built For Success

Get Success Results:

220 Principles That The Successful Use To Become Wildly Successful and How You Can Too

Learn the secrets and habits of the most successful people in the world and how you too can develop the right habits for success so you can live the life you've always wanted...

www.ShapleighPublishing.com/GetSuccessResultsBook

Table of Contents

Introduction

I want to thank you and congratulate you for purchasing the book, "The 7 Laws Of Motivation: Explode Your Motivation And Create A Mindset Built For Success." The book in your hands holds some valuable information that can put you on the right track towards getting and staying motivated. The idea is that with motivation, you can ultimately change your life.

Motivation is a vital part of life. Without motivation, you may never take the time to get up and do something with your life. Without motivation, you may never get the courage to chase your dreams. This would be a tragedy to anyone's life.

By definition, motivation is one or more reasons why a person may act or behave a certain way, in an effort to acquire something. Motivation is also the general want or need of someone to get something done. Being motivated can help you change your life one step at a time. Motivation also helps you to commit yourself to your mission of acquiring your heart's desire.

Motivation is a topic that is often discussed. People even dedicate their career's work towards understanding, developing and creating the model for motivation theory.

"The 7 Laws Of Motivation: Explode Your Motivation And Create A Mindset Built For Success," contains proven steps and strategies that will teach you how to become more motivated. It will also teach you how to restructure your mindset in order to thrive. There are plenty of books that provide you with vague steps to reach a higher level, but with this book, you will be given detailed steps that will ultimately change your life. It is my hope that this book offers youinsight into how to move forward and consistently stay motivated. With consistent implementation of these laws of motivation, you will see the results of accomplished goals, everywhere.

Thanks again for purchasing this book, I hope you enjoy it!

1st Law of Motivation: Without This There Is No Motivation

For anything that your heart desires, the journey to acquire it will never be an easy one. Plenty of people encounter ups and downs during the course of their journeys, but everyone reacts to it differently. Some of these people may keep going, but most will give up before they can attain their goals. This often happens when they are close to acquiring their goals as well. How would you feel if you'd quit before you'd accomplished something, not knowing that if you'd kept trying, your life would have been changed soon? That would definitely bring you down, wouldn't it?

Motivation is something that we often hear about, but it is so common, the definition is often assumed, and never confirmed. How is motivation defined? Motivation is what drives a person to move forward and put action towards making their goals happen. Motivation, as well as being self-motivated, is an important aspect of everyone's life. Knowing and understanding motivation, also pushes the agenda of wanting to pursue self-development, as well as carefully considering goals and reasons for them. When a person is motivated, they are void of stagnant behaviors. They are constantly on a quest to achieve something better. So, with that being said, we bring you to our first law of motivation.

The first law of motivation is all about your purpose and why you feel you want something in your life. Without a purpose or reason, there is no motivation. Knowing what your heart desires is a great first step, but when you know your purpose and your reason, you become able to set goals that will help you to acquire it all. Simply knowing what you want isn't the most important aspect of beginning your journey. You must not only know what you want, but you must also know why you want it. When you know why you want something, you will never forget why it is so important to you, and this can serve as great motivation over time. Knowing your purpose is the key to finding and keeping you motivated.

It is important to stay motivated because your actions will ultimately define how you will get to your wants and needs. When your desire falters, you will find that it is much harder to attain what you'd like. The reason you want something can alter your level of desire. Doing something for your loved ones can instantly push the envelope, and push you to accomplish things at a greater rate than you'd do for say, yourself. This is not to say that you wanting it for your own reasons aren't purpose enough. It's a must that you dig deep and channel your emotions, in order to find the fuel you need to move forward.

When you are certain of the reason behind your mission, you may encounter temporary emotions that can help you like putting a pair of batteries in your back, ultimately pushing you into action. As mentioned before, the right purpose will offer you motivation for periods of time. This is needed because there aren't too many goals that are accomplished overnight.

It has been found that motivation is an essential part of emotional intelligence, which is an important part of the concept of motivation. Emotional intelligence makes up one of the three areas of personal skills.

There are plenty of intellectuals that have dedicated their careers towards understanding motivation and its operation. One such individual is Daniel Goleman. He is the author of various books that discuss the topic of Emotional Intelligence. Within his research, he has found that there are four elements that motivation is comprised of. These elements are commitment, personal drive, initiative, and optimism.

Commitment

When commitment is considered, it is basically the dedication you have put forth towards your organizational or personal goals. Without dedication, whatever you want would be a fleeting desire that you'd never fully accomplish. When you commit to something, you are guaranteeing that you will see whatever it is through to the end. This is why commitment has made its place as one of the necessary elements that make up motivation. If you are not committed to see that something happens, then you actually lack the primary aspect of motivation.

Personal drive

Personal drive is your will to accomplish and acquire whatever ever it is that you want. Personal drive is your will to push yourself. Personal drive pushes you to improve your standard of efforts towards your goals. Are you actually getting out there and getting it done, or do you wait until the right time. Personal drive is your constant will that never falters. Without personal drive, along with commitment, you could and probably will throw in the towel prematurely.

Initiative

Initiative is the amount of effort you put in, towards achieving your goals. Initiative is how ready someone is to act on any particular opportunity at any given moment and describes what someone is willing to do to attain the goals they have set forth. Do you feel some actions are beneath you? Do you have the "do whatever it takes" mentality? If you do not take the initiative, no matter how big, or how small, you won't move any closer to your goals. Without initiative, you won't see any results.

Optimism

A large part of staying motivated is staying positive. This will be discussed in depth later in this book. However, optimism is defined as, "hopefulness and confidence," towards anything in your life, be it your future, or the need for a successful outcome, no matter what it may be. With optimism, you are often more likely to keep moving forward. An optimistic person has the ability to look past the setbacks along the journey, and keep moving forward in an effort to achieve their goals. When a person looks at their setbacks as learning lessons, they won't be affected as much. Their commitment, personal drive and initiative will remain intact, as well as their positive perspective.

Goleman also pointed out that a person that is motivated experiences a lot of perks. You will find that someone who is motivated, is more likely to be more organized, have more confidence and self-esteem, as well as possess great time-management skills. A person that is motivated doesn't doubt that whatever they want can happen. They know that it will for a fact. When you understand motivation and how important it is, you will begin to work towards developing the trait, in an effort to change the circumstances of your life. This is a great and powerful thing.

You need your motivation. There will be hard times that will arise, and they will leave you feeling defeated. It is in these moments of your journey that you will need to know your reasons, and you will need to tap into your motivation. It would be a good idea to write out your reasons. You should have an open mind, as you consider your reasons. By jotting down your reasons, you will always have them accessible when you need to reference them in times of setbacks. It is vital that you figure out these reasons because you need purpose behind you.

Aside from writing your reasons down, it is a good idea to visualize your reasons. Whether it's your family members, friends or even yourself, it is a great idea to take the time to visualize your reasons. Some people may find that their reasons have little to do with what they really want, and what this will do is help you to restructure your wants and your needs.

When you need help visualizing your reasons, keep photos of the loved ones that serve as your reason close by. Keep photos of whatever your reasons may be. Whatever you think will make you want to get up and work towards your dream, you make sure that you always have the visual available so that visualization will be easy. Visualization will come up again later in this book.

Visualization is such an important part of knowing your purpose. It is believed that visualization taps into the emotional aspects of your psyche. These visualizations will pose as a trigger. It doesn't matter what state you're in emotionally, your mind cannot differentiate between whether you are viewing it in person with your own two eyes, or if you visualize it in your mind. Either way, it serves as a trigger to motivate you.

When you take the time to visualize your purpose daily, you will be provided with the needed boost of motivation. These visualizations aid in helping you to propel forward, towards your goals. Taking the time out to consider and dwell on your purpose, will help you to ultimately move into action.

2nd Law of Motivation: If You Combine Your "Why" With This "What," You'll Be On Your Way!

If you didn't have a goal, what would you need motivation for? Motivation requires a goal. Motivation without a goal is like cereal without milk. It's a pointless existence. As mentioned before, motivation is a reason or reasons why a person may act or behave a certain way. Motivation is your reminder that you have something to do and should do it as soon as possible.

When you think of motivation and a goal, think of it as a cause and effect. Motivation causes you to reach your goal, which is the effect. There wouldn't be a need for motivation if you did not have your heart and eyes set on a particular goal. Without a goal, what would you need to be motivated for? Where would your motivation be pushing you?

If you do not have any goals, you should consider goal setting. Goal setting is defined as the creation of a plan that is meant to guide a person or group towards achieving their goal, or acquiring their heart's desire. Goal setting is also supposed to motivate, and it often works. Seeing your goals listed out will stir an excitement in you that will make you want to spring into action.

It has been found that when you choose a goal that is particularly challenging, or can be considered difficult, it tends to improve your performance. Goals that are easy don't necessarily push you towards increased performance. This is not always the case, but it has surely been found to happen.

Another thing to consider is that it is important to set goals that are actually attainable. When you set forth a goal that you know you can achieve, you'll be more likely to get started. The mere fact that your goal setting could push you into action confirms that a goal is needed to feel motivated. Consider retail competitions amongst employees. It has been found that contests, competitions, and challenges have a positive affect on motivation in the workspace. It may have a lot to do with ego, but ego is enough purpose to push someone forward. Your reason for accomplishing something could ultimately be that you want to be better than everyone else. This is motivation enough. This is a sure fire example that setting a goal is enough to push you forward.

Many people operate with the mindset that the simpler the goal, the easier it is to attain, but you'll find that these are the same people that rarely meet their goals. You want to incorporate small and realistic goals into your life, but listing goals that are slightly challenging will offer a push. You acquire more growth from challenging yourself, rather than giving yourself the bare minimum to accomplish. By challenging yourself, you push yourself out of the realm of being average. Who doesn't want to fight against the odds and achieve something they wouldn't normally achieve? Who doesn't want to be greater than average? It may sound strange, but finding a nice balance between doable and challenging tasks is a great way to spark motivation.

Keep Your Attitude in Check

Part of moving forward while remaining motivated means that you must eliminate your battle with procrastination and laziness. Getting rid of your lazy attitude is the first step towards staying motivated and getting things done. Mark Twain once said, "The secret of getting ahead is getting started." A person that adopts a productive attitude and focuses their attention on their work ethic will ultimately move closer towards their goals. It is best to adopt a mentality that is comprised of giving their mission their all, day in and day out. Consistency is always key.

Eliminating a lazy attitude goes hand in hand with initiative. When you adopt a mentality that is focused on being productive, you get way more accomplished. This goes back to initiative. A little initiative goes a very long way. This is due to the fact that, you put in much more effort when you get rid of a lazy mindset. This is one of the most important parts of staying motivated. Try waking up earlier and creating a to-do list for reference. This will aid in keeping a productive attitude. Every time you knock something off of your list, you will want to get started on the next part of the list.

Visualize

Another method to consider when trying to implement motivation law number two is to constantly visualize your goals everyday. We discussed this earlier in the first chapter. This is a great way to stay motivated. It's true that you must have an idea or a vision of what your goal looks like before you can actually believe in it or feel motivated to accomplish it. This coincides with the well-known adage, "seeing is believing".

Visualizing is a technique that is meant to help create mental images of events that will take place in the future whether it's losing weight, winning an award or anything else of that nature. You should use visualization not only to remind yourself of what you want but also to remind yourself why you want it.When a person takes out the time to visualize what it is that they want, they will often find it easier to believe that there is a chance they can achieve whatever it is that they want to achieve. A person will find that by visualizing their goal, they felt more motivated and prepared to pursue their goals.

Many people hear visualization and assume that it is the "think it, and you will be it" mentality. It isn't as simple as that. That ideology is very unrealistic. You must always partner visualization with hard work. When visualization is suggested, the idea is that if you can picture what you want happening, you will probably want it more, and therefore, you will work harder to achieve it. Visualization isn't a made up gimmick. Visualization is much more than dreaming, hoping and wishing. Visualization is a method that has been well developed, and has also been proven to improve performance. This is also supported by scientific evidence that has been used by many people that are highly motivated and very successful. These people that use visualization to be motivated are in plenty of fields and industries, so it's safe to say that visualization works for any and every goal, no matter what it pertains to.

Athletes are a great example of successful people who live by the visualization method. Studies have shown that visualization increases athletic performance by improving coordination, motivation, and concentration. Visualization also helps with relaxation and helps to reduce fear and anxiety. This goes hand in hand with how a goal can be so intimidating that a person doesn't go out to get it. When you visualize your dreams and goals, you eliminate that anxiety.

Many people don't understand how visualization works. Research suggests using brain imagery and visualization works because neurons in our brains, which are those electrically excitable cells that transmit information, understand imagery as being equal to real-life action. When a person visualizes an act, the brain puts out an impulse that tells your neurons to "perform" the action. This then creates a new neural pathway — which is a clusters of cells in our brain that work together to make memories or create learned behaviors. This gets our bodies ready to act in ways that are consistent to what has been imagined.

So, to implement motivational law number two, you must set goals, get rid of your lazy attitude, and visualize your goals. When you add these tools to your arsenal, you will be on the fast track to staying motivated and accomplishing your goals.

3rd Law of Motivation: This Is The #1 Secret Of Motivation And Success

Timelines are the worst thing when it comes to matters of your life. You can set your intentions and set your goals, but you can't necessarily dictate when things will take place. If you're anything like me, you may find it discouraging when you aren't able to accomplish things exactly when you would like to. You may feel as if you aren't doing enough. As discussed earlier. The smallest bit of initiative will give you a lot of results, you just have to get it done.

Little do you know, small steps are just enough to move you closer to your dreams bit by bit. The only thing is, you must continue to put forth these small actions on a consistent basis. It is only through consistency that you will move closer to the goals you are trying to accomplish. Over time, your results will be incredible, and you will find yourself surprised by them.

When you have an issue achieving big goal, it may be a good idea to break your goals into smaller goals or steps. A baby step is a step nonetheless. Deliberately making an effort to break things into segments that make you comfortable will allow you to feel much more motivated. This is due to the fact that you prevent yourself from being overwhelmed.

The Slight Edge and The Compound Effect

One method to consider when breaking your goals into smaller pieces is the slight edge and the compound effect. Both ideas were written about by Jeff Olsen and Darren Hardy, respectively. When you're trying to change your life, it's a good idea to get a slight edge in your life. To get a slight edge in your life, it is a good idea to take small actions, consistently over time. In theory, everyone's lives, from beginning to end are comprised of what is called the slight edge. Their lives are made up of thousands of actions that pile up over time. This is as a result of these actions being repeated day in and day out.

When you couple positive attitudes with positive efforts daily, you are matched with what is called the compound effect. The compound effect is basically an action plus another action, equaling two other actions over a period of time. This is due to each of the actions working off of one another. This creates a multiplying effect rather than an adding one.

The idea is to start considering each of your actions in terms of multiplication. However, in doing it this way, you must also be consistent in your efforts. Without consistency, every movement is made in vain. With consistency, your actions will multiply into the results you desire. In a nutshell, the slight edge transforms into compounding efforts. With these two elements, you will be able to achieve the success you want.

When it comes to staying motivated, patience is a virtue. You must be committed to putting the time in. With that being said, time is of the essence. It is always ticking away, and it pauses for no one. Your time is valuable, and you must never forget that. Time can never be rewound. You can never get your moments back, so you must constantly take advantage of your time. None of your time should ever be wasted. If you do not take advantage of your time, it will ultimately work against you. When you put in effort every day, as well as when you take actions everyday, you are ensuring that you are moving closer to your goals. Eliminate the excuses and move forward.

When you are stagnant and aren't putting forth effort, you lose motivation. When you make it routine to work towards your goal by staying in an action, you will ensure motivation. When you get in the habit of working towards your goals, this action itself will help you to push you forward. The more effort you put into your actions, the more likely you are able to achieve your goals. When you put forth actions, there's no way you won't experience results.

If you aren't sure of how to move forward or even start for that matter, take the time to start small. The slightest action is an action nonetheless. This fact can't be stressed enough. Take action daily and consistently.

4th Law of Motivation: These Are Little Volts Of Motivation To Help You On Your Journey

Who doesn't like rewards? Who wouldn't want to be rewarded for efforts? When you have something to look forward to acquiring, aside from your goals, that will definitely push you to perform. A reward at the end of the day is more than enough to motivate someone to work hard and push forward towards their goals. There isn't anything wrong with rewarding yourself. You must reward yourself, and do so on a regular basis. If you are consist and constantly putting forth effort you deserve to be rewarded.

While recognition is important, rewards are just as essential. Recognition and praise for accomplishing certain goals can be considered to have a limited shelf life. You will find that at a certain point in your journey, you will have to put your money where your mouth is. You must eventually reward yourself and others in an effort to give shine to results that can be deemed superior.

You can use rewards to motivate yourself, and you can use these same rewards to motivate others. This will be discussed further in later chapters. Rewards should also come after extra effort has been put forth. Just as anyone else would, enthusiasm will be lost when you begin to feel as though there isn't anything to look forward to. A guaranteed payoff is always enough to keep someone feeling enthusiastic

When you reward yourself, you shouldn't limit it to only being rewarded for longer-term goals. Consider how we suggested breaking big goals up into smaller actions. You should be the same way when it comes to you rewarding yourself. With each of the smaller goals that you accomplish, you should reward yourself the same way.

Anything can be considered a reward. Rewards can come in various shapes and sizes. They can even be tangible or intangible. When you consider tangible rewards, you should always include such things as treats, gift certificates, a shopping spree, or an adventure. Whatever you deem appropriate, is what you should consider rewarding yourself with.

Intangible rewards are a different story. Intangible rewards can be just as effective in motivating yourself and your peers, as a tangible reward would. Something as simple as taking a friend out to experience something new can have a huge impact.

One of the most effective things to do in regard to rewards is to connect rewards to the completion of a specific task. Also, be sure to make these rewards special and a one-time event so that it doesn't downgrade its value as a sufficient reward. As mentioned before, short-term rewards are just as motivating as rewards you acquire once you have accomplished a long-term goal.

Try making a list. We've discussed making lists before when we talked about goal setting. As you make this list of goals, you should partner each goal with a reward that you deem appropriate. Your reward can be anything you choose but consider the following:

1. Your reward must be proportionate to the goal that you have listed. For example, don't pull out all the stops for not eating junk for a week. It wouldn't make sense to by yourself a new car for losing five pounds. Another example of a bad reward would be a luxury trip to Europe, for running a mile in under ten minutes. A more appropriate reward would actually be treating yourself to a new outfit after refraining from eating junk food and dropping a pants size.

2. It is important to not choose rewards that are counter-productive. Take the same goal as above. If you lose five pounds and drop a pants size, it isn't a good idea to binge eat French fries and other junk foods. This would be a reward that ultimately gives you a setback. Setbacks are inevitable, but when you do it to yourself, it could have been avoided. Self-sabotage is not a good idea.

Recognition is another aspect of motivation that is important. If you put forth effort and never receive any recognition, you will find yourself unmotivated. Everyone wants to know that someone has noticed that they are putting in effort. Yes, you can give you self-recognition, but it is more efficient when you receive that external recognition.

The power of recognition is a very powerful one. It is another tool to equip yourself with. It is vital to keep yourself and people around you motivated. However, you must give recognition in moderation. If you do it too often, you and others may become numb to it. This will, in turn, eliminate the motivation factor.

When a person receives recognition for their accomplishments, this heightens the value they place on their goal. People typically do their best when they know that someone else is looking. The want to impress is motivation enough. Motivation sets this aspect into motion. A little recognition goes a long way.

5th Law of Motivation: These Are Powerful Forces Of Natural Motivation

As a human being, and especially if you are an extrovert, you typically want to be surrounded by others. Friends and often family are our comfort systems, but many people take for granted that who you surround yourself with has a great affect on who you are and who you become.

Journal of Consumer Research published a study in 2014 that discussed the fact that moral support is commonly provided with the bonds of friendship. With the support of a friendship, it is hoped that the moral support will prevent you from delving into the counter-productive realm of temptation. The bonds of friendship can also push you into activities that you wouldn't normally be apart of. It is known that friends can often conspire together, experiencing sketchy indulgences, whenever they choose.

Researchers have also found that partners are more likely to become partners in crime, rather than to stop you from partaking in the negative indulges. Indulging together isn't always the safest thing. In reality, it's hard to avoid the comfort of doing something in a group. Picking friends that make terrible decisions isn't a good idea. You are who you hang with and if you surround yourself with people who make poor choices, you risk the chance of being pulled down, in a negative way. Choosing people that inspire and challenge you for the better is very important. Surrounding yourself with inspiring people will bring you that much closer to achieving your goals.

It is especially important to be careful when choosing your friends because everyone isn't your friend. Sometimes the people who latch on to you have ulterior motives. Their ulterior motives may be dedicated solely to bringing you down. A person with such negative intentions will do anything in their power to prevent you from moving in a positive direction. They will encourage behaviors that have negative affects on you. If you aren't a person who is strong willed, you will find yourself blinded by their false friendship. This is a terrible thing to find yourself a part of.

Friendship and groups are never a bad thing. You just have to be careful with how you chose them. Take your time in surrounding yourself with positive people. The search is worth it. The sense of belonging to a group can ultimately motivate you if you surround yourself with the right types of people. If you don't choose the right people, it could possibly demotivate you. This is especially true if the group is made up of negative people.

You will find a few tips to help you choose your friends much wiser below:

Associate yourself with people who are on a level higher than yours.

If your goal consists of focusing on taking your business, career, or life to the next level, then it's a good idea to connect yourself with people on that next level. Networking is key. Not only will you be motivated by their accomplishments, but also you will find yourself working towards matching your counterpart's efforts. When you connect with people who are more accomplished, you will also help expand your mind to considering and thinking of greater possibilities. Naturally, people are more comfortable when they are in a place with counterparts that are like themselves. This is normal and quite okay. It's always a good idea to step out of your comfort zone. When you step out of your comfort zone and spend time with people who can expose you to greater things, new information and a higher level of living; you will inevitably find yourself much more motivated. Valuing these friendships will result in you advancing or at least encountering results that will help push you forward.

Similar values are vital to choosing friends.

It's normal to believe that diversity is a great way to choose your friends. In many ways, this is true, but friendships work much better when you have things in common. It's best to keep core friendships with like-minded people, especially when it comes to your general values and beliefs. You can always respect the opinions and differences of others, but choosing your friends based on the fact that they hold similar values to yours, will also keep you from compromising or being negatively influenced by those people that don't uphold your same values and the standards that you operate your life by. Friends that have similar values or beliefs can ultimately force each other to stay accountable. This is a very important aspect of choosing friends.

Friends with a common goal are important.

Friends should be known as your purpose partners. They help you push forward towards your mission. Having friends with common goals, particularly when you are an entrepreneur, can help you to push each other. You'll find that you can work on your goals as a team and eventually encourage each other to reach them.

Choose your friends so that they balance you out.

It's a great idea to choose your friends based on what they are better at than you. When you choose your friends based on their strengths that you don't necessarily have, you find a balance that is needed. Everyone is made up of strengths and weaknesses, and at some point, you will know exactly what yours are.

When you choose the right friends, you can tap into the skills, talents, and abilities of your friends that have expertise in areas that you don't. Allow your friends to help you alter your weaknesses. Consider the following:

Your weaknesses could consist of not being great at keeping your closet organized, you could enlist your friends as help. What if you were a great writer, you could offer assistance to a friend that is updating her resume or working on a book. When you capitalize on each other's strengths, you'll find that everyone involved wins.

A friend that motivates and encourages is vital.

You and others have a lot of important responsibilities when it comes to being a great friend. One thing to consider when choosing a friend is to choose those that not only push you but to also encourage and motivate you. Friends that do this are the best purpose partners you could ask for. You don't want a friend that has a negative attitude or is down in the dumps all the time. No one does. The people that are uplifting and positive are naturally who we should want to be around. Consider what categories your friends fall under? Think about the subject content of your conversations with these friends? The best types of friends are those that will be there to give you a listening ear. This will help you to look at your situation in a positive way.

A friend that shares the same interest is a great idea.

When you choose your friends, you should look for people that share the same interests. Life is much more fun when you have friends that have similar interests. With a friend that shares the same interests, you can find yourself enjoying outings and other activities together. You can choose from sports, music, performing arts or even food. It's understood that when you share interests with others, you have someone to call on when you need camaraderie and friendship. With a friend with the same interests, you have someone to visit new places and experience new things with.

Find friends that crave knowledge.

You should always consider choosing friends that have a thirst for knowledge. Someone who always wants to learn more is typically a person that is highly motivated. One of the most important parts of life is learning, growing and advancing. You should make it a point to constantly be learning. We discussed this before. Learning will give you the boost of motivation you may need because you find yourself feeling more equipped. When you choose friends that like to learn, you will find that you can learn from each other. This is always a good thing because you will have a friend who can recommend a good book or share information with you that will either help motivate you to put you on a path toward accomplishing your goal. A friend that is an avid reader or constantly on the quest for knowledge will usually be great conversationalist who challenge your mind while you're having fun.

A purpose partner is the best friend you can ask for.

When you choose your friends, you want someone that you know will push harder for your mission than you would. When you think of your friends as a purpose partner, you look at them as someone who you can share your goals and dreams with, without worries. You trust them, and you know that they will help motivate and encourage you. They will make it their mission to keep pushing you toward accomplishing each and every one of your goals. When you discuss your plans with your friend or your purpose partners, you will find that they not only help you stay accountable to following through, but they will make sure that they see to it. It becomes your job to make sure that you give them the opportunity to actually help you.

A friend that celebrates yours success is a real friend.

We will discuss why this is so important later in the book, but it is definitely a great idea to choose friends that will not only celebrate your success but also will be genuinely happy for you. It is in your best interest to pick friends that don't just tolerate you, but also celebrate you and your accomplishments as if they were their own.

A person that is your true friend won't envy. A true friend will celebrate every milestone, accomplishment and success story on your journey, no matter how his or her life journey is going. A true friend won't compare themselves to you and your journey. They will simply rejoice in your greatness. You will only encounter genuine happiness from them, whenever they see you succeed. They will also be the first person to tell you "congratulations!" These types of friends are rare and can be hard to find, but when you find them, it is in your best interest to keep them close!

When you choose your friends wisely, you will not only find yourself feeling supported, but you will also find yourself consistently motivated and ready to move towards your goals.

6th Law of Motivation; This Will Better Prepare You For Your Journey To Success And Accomplishment

Positive vibes are essential to creating a great life. Positive attitudes are a critical part of being motivated and staying motivated. Whatever you think about, will manifest itself in your world. You must remain positive consistently in order to continue on the right path. Being positive will help you move forward, without considering quitting. Remaining positive will also help you to look on the bright side, which is vital to overcoming the many setbacks that will occur during your journey.

Why is positive thinking so important? Recent research has found that positive thinking isn't solely about being happy at all times, or showing that you are in a good mood all the time. There is much more to the idea of positive thinking. Positive thinking can actually create real value in your life and ultimately help you to either build or improve on skills that last much longer than a smile would. Positive thinking has a good affect on everything from your health to your work and your life as a whole.

Psychological researcher at the University of North Carolina, Barbara Fredrickson has authored work that offers surprising insight into positive thinking and how it changes your skill set.

Fredrickson has dedicated a lot of her career towards highlighting empowering methods to stay positive. In her research, she tested how positive emotions affect the brain. These tests were accomplished by setting up various small experiments, in which Fredrickson divided her research subjects into 5 groups. Each of the five groups were shown a different film clip that provoked various emotions.

The idea was that every clip would pull out different emotions from the subjects in each group. The first two groups were shown clips that provoked positive emotions. Joy was the emotion that was created for the first group. The second group viewed images that created feelings of contentment. Neutral images were viewed by the third group, and basically, there weren't any significant images to speak of.

The last two groups were shown clips that were meant to provoke emotions that were more on the negative spectrum. Group four was subjected to images that provoked emotions of fear. The fifth group viewed images that provoked feelings of anger.

When all of the groups finished viewing their clips, each of them were asked to imagine themselves in a scenario where these same feelings would arise. The participants were then asked to write down what they would do in these same situations. Next, each of the participants were given a piece of paper with 20 blank lines on it. Each line began with the phrase, "I would like to..."

Out of all the participants, those who saw images of anger and fear wrote down the fewest responses. However, those participants that saw images of joy and contentment wrote down a substantially higher number of actions that they would take. This is also true when these participants were compared to the neutral group.

This shows that, whenever someone is experiencing positive emotions like joy, contentment, and love, they will see more possibilities in their life. Fredrickson's findings are among the first findings that showed that positive emotions broaden your sense of possibility and open your mind up to more options. In turn, you will feel much more motivated to move forward and achieve your goals.

A person that is equipped with a positive attitude often feels less discouraged. Those that feel less discouraged are less likely to quit. It cannot be reiterated enough that there will be a lot of bumps in the road. Setbacks are part of the journey. They can't be avoided. In order to persevere, you must adopt an attitude that is positive. Staying positive is one of the most important aspects of staying motivated.

Staying positive isn't as easy as it sounds. It takes constant effort, and you'll find that it may be hard to stay consistent. There are plenty of things that can be done to help you stay positive. A few of the suggestions are below:

Never Compare Yourself to Others

Every time you compare yourself to the next person, you will lose. You'll find that in worrying about someone else, you neglect to focus on your own agenda, which in turn can result in many setbacks for you. When you constantly compare yourself to others, you will more than likely feel as though you are less than them. This is due to you underrating yourself while primping up their scores. It is more than likely that you will end up on the losing side of the comparison. It sounds mean, buts it's just being honest. In focusing on what the other person is and isn't, you will surely be kept from figuring out who you are and what you want to become. There will always be someone that has done more than you, but there will always be someone that has done more than him or her. It's inevitable. You can't avoid being the person that is less accomplished. It will happen on and on throughout your life.

When you compare yourself to other people, you will eventually begin to sulk. It is a downward spiral from there. You will find it difficult to draw the line. When should you stop comparing yourself? There won't be anymore self-control. How do you even start the comparison? What is it based on? It doesn't make sense to judge yourself based on someone else's dream. It isn't smart to compare two things that aren't relatable. Consider this, would you compare only matters such as career-related achievements, such as job titles, compensation, business travel locations, number of direct reports, perks, and benefits, or would you judge them on whether they have an office with a door or limited to working in a tiny cubicle? If you focus on how things should be compared, you may consider whether you would compare personal accomplishments, such as who owns the most expensive car, the biggest house, got married first, went to the coolest place for their honeymoon? When you are constantly comparing yourself to others, you are ultimately pushing yourself down a long rabbit hole. Think about it this way, would you judge a fish on its flying skills? You wouldn't because fish don't fly. In other words, you are the person you are for a reason. The person you get the urge to pit yourself up against is who they are for their reason. Everyone experiences different things throughout their lives, for their own reason. Comparing things that are in different class sets, for example, doesn't make sense.

Remember you are one of a Kind

There is no one on this earth that is exactly like you. This is because you are uniquely special. You will never be the replica of another person. Being a copycat isn't acceptable. All things considered, if you were a genetic twin to another person, they wouldn't grow up to have the exact same experiences, ideas, activities, thoughts or even influences. Each of your personalities would differ substantially. The two of you probably wouldn't even have the same likes or dislikes. You would more than likely differ substantially.

With all of this considered, this is exactly why you should never compare yourself to the next person. It wouldn't make sense for you to be the same room as a person with differing personal and career achievements. There wouldn't be any room to connect. As you move forward, it is your best bet for you to see everyone as a separate person that is unique. You will never be them, and they will never be you.

Conscious Effort Counts

Just as it's hard to constantly stay positive, it's not always easy to not compare yourself to others. When you take the time to make a conscious effort to not compare yourself to others, it will eventually become a learned habit. Take the time to celebrate your uniqueness. Rejoice in the things that make you different from others. Celebrate you own journey and your own accomplishments. It doesn't matter when these accomplishments occur. Remember you are on your own timeline. When you eliminate anxiety and refuse to compare yourself to others, this is when you will find that you thrive better.

Never Compare, Always Congratulate

Comparing yourself to others often comes with an envious attitude. Take the time to teach yourself how to celebrate and rejoice in the accomplishments of not only yourself but of others. Are you genuinely happy for your loved ones when they share something awesome with you? Be it a coworker, family member or friend; are you genuinely excited for them, or are do you feel slighted that it wasn't you?

For some people, jealousy and feeling inadequate are unavoidable emotions, but these are feelings that you should avoid. Transform those emotions into feelings that are more positive in nature. Rejoice in their excitement and celebrate their accomplishments. There isn't anything wrong with being happy for the people around you. Give your encouragement that is genuine and heartfelt. A simple congratulations works too. Rejoice in their news and make them feel amazing for accomplishing whatever it is that they accomplished.

A great example of this would be attending your college or high school reunion. You'll encounter a lot of old friends that you may have lost touch with. People will chat and catch up on their lives, and you'll probably find someone who you feel is living a much better life than you. Rather than be envious or filled with jealousy, you should be excited. Share your feeling of happiness and excitement with other people. Focus on the happiness and joy they are experiencing as a result of their accomplishments and connect based on that. You will be filled with a satisfaction that allows you to be happy for that other person.

One thing to consider when you feel the urge to compare yourself to someone else is that you don't know exactly what it took for him or her to get to where they are. A lot of tears and disappointment could have been in their journey. They could have spent tireless hours and nights to get to where they are, and you only see the glitz of their accomplishments. Sometimes achievement comes at the expense of strife, and this isn't necessarily something that they would have liked to experience. So, also, remember that you don't know what it took for them to get to where they are.

Why I suggest that you not look at another person's accomplishments and become envious, you should at least look at their accomplishments as a means for motivation. If there is something they have done that you wish you would have done, begin to take steps to accomplish it. This is the only way for you to get it done. You can even mirror your goal setting after their journey in an effort to figure out how to get what they have. Ask them questions if you must. Either way, you stifle yourself when you focus more on what the next person has rather than giving your own goals the attention that it needs.

Track Your Progress

You can become motivated by the progress of someone else, but you will find that you are more motivated by the progress you see in yourself. Tracking your progress and creating a goal traker is a great way for you to see your growth and rejoice in it. Track your progress religiously. You will begin to notice the small steps have amounted to unexpected results.

When you track your progress, you have a blueprint of your accomplishments to look back on. Information purposes isn't all that this tracking is for. If gives you the opportunity to look back at what you have accomplished, while taking note of trends and heights accomplished. This, in turn, will help motivate you towards your goals.

Diligently checking your progress daily will help you to take a step towards accomplishing your goals as well.

It is a good idea to start by creating a chart, in which you make "x" or dots every time you accomplish one of your steps. Gold stars are some people's marking of choice. The more you see these markings on your chart, the more you will want to acquire more markings that symbolize your progress. It's a helpful way of staying motivated. Whether it's a chart, a journal or a training log, the fact that your progress is documented, shows that you can actually get things done. It will serve as a reminder every time you feel as though you can't keep going. In charting your progress, you give yourself a sense of pride, every time you see a positive mark.

When you track your progress, keeping a daily journal of your goals is another way to track you progress, as well as shape your goals as they change. Consistently journaling your goals, as well as your progress can be a powerful motivator. When you write in your journal, you shouldn't have only what you did for the day, but you should also journal your thoughts about how it happened, how it made you feel, what mistakes you made, what things you could do to improve the next time. One suggestion that will help you to stay consistent about keeping a journalist to make sure you do it right after you accomplish your goal each day. Make it a point to keep a journal as a sensory pleasure.

It is important to be completely honest with yourself, as you document your progress. You do want to chart all of the great results you are acquiring, but you also want to document the setbacks. The idea behind this is to notice behaviors before they become habits. If you document trends that you may have been experiencing, you will ultimately begin to alter your behaviors to gain more progress, rather than setbacks. The negative markings aren't meant to discourage you. Don't let them keep you from moving forward. Remember with a positive attitude, setbacks become lessons learned. Do make a conscious effort to strive for good marks most of the time.

Attitude of Gratitude

When it comes to being and staying motivated, it is important to not to focus on what you don't have or what you haven't done. You must always take into consideration what you already have and how far you've already come. Be thankful for everything you have. Be grateful that you have come as far as you have.

When you have an attitude that takes note of everything that you already have, you will be able to rejoice in every bit of progress you experience. If you are thankful for what you have, you won't feel the need to compare yourself to others. You will rejoice in the things you have earned and acquired when you are thankful for all that you have.

Find Inspiration

To seek motivation, you must often seek inspiration. Seek inspiration often, it is a great part of staying motivated. Daily, immerse yourself in inspirational literature. Read positive quotes. Listen to music or speeches with positive messages. Find positive podcast and view positive media. Use the stories of others to inspire you on your journey by reading their biographies or success memoirs. It is important to eliminate any and all of the negative media you may typically come into contact with. It is also very important to remove negative people from your life as well.

It shouldn't be hard to find inspiration because it is everywhere. The smallest thing can inspire, it just depends on the person. One of the best motivators is inspiration. Seeking inspiration daily will assist you in sustaining motivation over the course of your long journey. Remember, inspiration can be found in the people you encounter and the places you go. You may also find that online success stories, forums, blogs, quotes, books, family and friends, music and photos are great sources of inspiration as well.

Motivate Others

Another way to stay motivated is to help others. When you help others, you will find that amazingly, you are motivated and encouraged. Using your own personal skill set and knowledge to lead them puts you in an invincible mindset. Helping another person can be a powerful motivator. This is especially true when you combine it with your reasons of "why" and your designated purpose. It is often forgotten that we are here in this life, to serve others for their betterment. Being motivated by the assistance is just a perk.

Motivating others is one of the best ways to help motivate yourself. Helping others succeed is an amazing feeling that eventually pushes you towards your goals. Who doesn't see the success of another person and feel like working hard towards their own successes? The urge for success is very contagious. It will inevitably rub off on you.

When you put forth effort towards helping someone else, this requires focus and attention. Realistically focus and attention are vital components of motivation in general. Helping another person shows that you can accomplish something. Helping someone else succeed should instantly tell you that you can do the same for yourself. Helping yourself should actually be easier.

When you become motivated by the people you have helped, you will feel as though you are refocused and will ultimately put more attention towards achieving the necessary outcome. It is important to consider how motivating yourself and motivating others is one in the same.

Something to take into consideration, is who are you motivating? Take a moment to consider the type of people you plan to assist in their quest for motivation. You don't have to be a supervisor in order to motivate other people. There are plenty of people that are all around us, who are looking for a little inspiration or motivation. You can motivate other people with ease, you just have to try. Your mission is to make an effort to motivate other people daily. Don't do it every other week or every other month. Take the time to motivate someone each day. The more often you motivate others, the more likely you are to wind up motivating yourself.

Create a Positive Environment for Yourself and Others

While motivating others is suggested, it is ultimately means that you help to create a place where the person can eventually motivate themselves. If no one tries to motivate anyone, then no one is motivated. It is important that you become motivated so that it may ultimately become contagious. People will ultimately begin to not only motivate themselves but others as well.

Start by focusing your efforts on creating an environment that is positive, or at least helpful. This can be done, by having a positive outlook and looking at what is possible. Avoid the negative and the naysayer comments of other people, they obviously haven't grasped the concept of inspiring and encouraging others. When you help others, you will begin to adopt a positive attitude and you will begin to not only envision the possible but also believe that it can happen. In reality, it will be hard for you to not believe it could happen for yourself as well.

Positive environments are contagious. You want other people to want to pass on their motivation. People who allow themselves to be open to the possibilities will ultimately become more focused on having a more positive attitude while being more focused on achieving what others may think or believe is impossible. Remember that your mission is a very simple one. When you motivate others, you not only motivate yourself, but you encourage them to go out and motivate others. It's a domino affect that leads to everyone paying it forward.

7th Law of Motivation: The Real Purpose And Desire Of Motivation

The real purpose and reason for motivation is learning. Everyone must immerse himself or herself in whatever it is that they want to achieve. It is important to learn at a speed that is insatiable. This is important, because the more you know, the less you will be intimidated by your goals.

With knowledge, you equip yourself with the needed information to improve your skill set. When your skill set is improved, you have equipped yourself with the weapons you need to achieve whatever you desire. A challenge won't seem like a challenge any longer. You will find motivation in your confidence because you won't be afraid to try. When you set forth a goal that you know you can achieve, you'll be more likely to get started, and in most cases, you'll be more likely to actually acquire what it is that you desire.

Learning about the subject surrounding your goal isn't the only learning that is important. Yes, you should immerse yourself in whatever subject pertains to your goals, but you should also take the time to learn about yourself. In all actuality, learning about yourself is one of the hardest things to avoid when you are trying to stay motivated and achieve a goal.

To learn more about yourself, you must ask yourself the tough and important questions. What do you want? Why do you want it? When do you want it? Is this really what you want? You can get lost in the abundance of questions that come to mind. Many times, learning about yourself is a trial and error process, and that is okay. As you learn and fail it is easy to get discouraged, but if you take the time to look on the bright side, you will find that you are learning not only about your weaknesses, but you will also be able to pinpoint your strengths. Knowing what you are strong at, will also serve as much needed motivation.

As you encounter setbacks and achievements, there will be plenty of times where you are ready to give up and walk away. Staying positive and patient is essential to moving forward and achieving your goals. Your success isn't on the timeline you create, you have to simply endure, fight the urges to quit and continue moving forward. It may even be a good idea to expect the best but prepare for the worse. This way, you can get your mind acclimated with the idea that you can fail once, twice, or even multiple times. This does not mean that you will never achieve your goal, and this is one of the most important things to remember.

As you learn about yourself, you will find that some of your goals weren't really what you wanted. You will begin to refine your goals. This is an important thing. Knowing these things will allow you to move forward, consciously putting forth consistent effort that speaks to who you are as a person. When you are consistently making moves that speak to your true self, you will be that much closer to moving towards the person you want to be. This will help motivate you because you will begin to strive harder for what you want to become.

We've discussed motivation in its entirety, starting out with creating goals and figuring out what works best to motivate you. If you've begun to apply this law in an effort to change your life, or achieve your goals; you've probably learned a lot about yourself.

Learning about yourself is one of the most amazing perks that comes along with motivation. No one really knows what they want until they sit down and actually take into consideration their wants and needs. You also learn a lot about yourself when you see how you react to not only the achievements but the setbacks as well. A person that goes out to achieve their goals is fearless and this is something to be proud of.

The whole point of finding your motivation is to not only learn things about yourself that are usually taken for granted but also to challenge yourself. It is here that you learn how you operate when facing a challenge, and that's important weapon to have in your arsenal of traits.

It is true that staying motivated can be difficult at times. This is only due to the fact that the process of finding motivation is mainly about personal growth and forcing yourself to become a better version than you were the day before. You must remember that finding and keeping motivated is a one day at a time kind of game, but it is vital to improving yourself for the better.

Motivation, as you may have realized is essential to pushing your agenda forward, no matter what it is that you need or want. The road to success is one that is full of bumps and curves, and many people aren't prepared for the setbacks they may experience along the way. A strong person will persevere and keep going. A weak person will accept defeat and give up, completely losing all motivation to attain their goal.

Every person with a dream or a goal should make it a point to never give up. Setbacks are a part of the journey, and they teach you lessons that you may have never learned if you hadn't tried. The best advice that can be given to anyone regarding motivation is to never give up and embrace the journey because this is what motivation is all about. Think of it this way, if you enjoy your journey blow for blow, you'll have plenty of memories to look back on once you've attained what you once believed was unattainable. You can even turn your journey into a testimony to motivate other people. Your life lessons can be the constant fuel for someone else in the same position. That's one of the secret's of motivation: it gives back in ways you never thought it would. Your experiences can help serve others who are in your same spot long after you've accomplished your goal.

Conclusion

Thank you again for purchasing this book!

I hope this book was able to help you to become motivated, as well as help you understand that motivation helps you to commit to your mission of acquiring your heart's desire.

This book contains proven steps and strategies on how to become more motivated as well as restructure your mindset in order to thrive. It is our hope that we have surpassed your expectations. Hopefully, those that have dedicated their career's work towards understanding, developing and creating the model for the motivation theory, have provided you with enough information to move you towards your goals. It is my hope that this book has offeredinsight into how to move forward and consistently stay motivated.

Everyone is wired differently, so it is now your job to apply these laws to your life in an effort to spark change. Your next step is to figure out your heart's desire and set goals. Remember, without a goal, there wouldn't be a need for motivation. You must learn to stay patient. Give yourself an opportunity to grow by perfecting your craft and constantly immersing yourself in learning more about your craft. Maintain a positive attitude and have a perspective that looks at setbacks as a learning lesson. Surround yourself with people that motivate you. Steer clear of comparing yourself to others, and actually take the time to motivate others in an effort to motivate yourself. If you feel overwhelmed, simply take it one step at a time.

Finally, if you enjoyed this book, then I'd like to ask you for a favor, would you be kind enough to leave a review for this book on Amazon? It'd be greatly appreciated!

Thank you and good luck!

P.S-Don't forget to check out your FREE BONUS on the next page! You won't want to miss out on it!

Also check out my other books from the "7 Laws" Series on success and personal growth on the last page!

FREE BONUS E-BOOK!

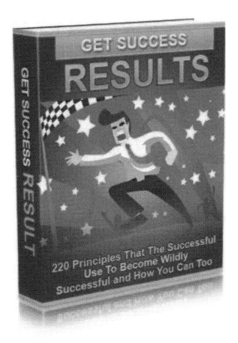

Get Success Results:

220 Principles That The Successful Use To Become Wildly Successful
and How You Can Too

Learn the secrets and habits of the most successful people in the world
and how you too can develop the right habits for success so you can
live the life you've always wanted...

www.ShapleighPublishing.com/GetSuccessResultsBook

OTHER BOOKS IN THE "7 LAWS" SERIES

Check out the current and the upcoming books in Brian Cagneey's "7 Laws" series on personal development and success!

amazon.com/author/briancagneey

The 7 Laws Of Habits: Using Habits To Achieve Success, Happiness, And Anything You Want!

The 7 Laws Of Motivation: Explode Your Motivation And Create A Mindset Built For Success

The 7 Laws Of Happiness: Using The Power Of Happiness To Create Amazing Results In Life!

The 7 Laws Of Productivity: 10X Your Success With Focus, Time Management, Self-Discipline, And Action.

The 7 Laws Of Fear: Break What's Holding You Back And Turn Fear Into Confidence.

The 7 Laws of Confidence: Feel Unstoppable, Destroy Doubt, And Accomplish Your Biggest Goals.

The 7 Laws Of Focus: Focus: The #1 Secret For Excellence, Productivity and Radical Results.

The 7 Laws Of Leadership: Develop Yourself, Influence Others And People Will Follow.

The 7 Laws of Communication: The Secrets Of Being Comfortable, Confident, And Unforgettable With Anyone!

The 7 Laws Of Self-Discipline: Become Strong, Become Confident And Create Your Success

The 7 Laws Of Coaching: Powerful Coaching Skills That Will Predict Your Team's Success

amazon.com/author/briancagneey

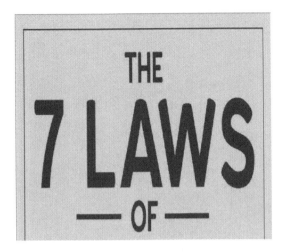

ABOUT BRIAN CAGNEEY

Brian Cagneey is the author of the well-known "7 Laws" book series on personal development. His books cover a wide range of topics including personal growth, habits, self-discipline, happiness, success, communication, leadership, coaching, motivation, confidence, fear, productivity, and focus.

Brian's mission is to renew people's minds and to help everyday, ordinary people become positive, successful, and mission driven. His passion for writing is fueled by the desire to see as many people as possible not just survive their life but thrive and excel.

Brian is an avid student of the laws of success. His beliefs on accomplishment are not based on theory, but real life practice. Brian knows that wisdom and knowledge are only half of the equation, the other half of success is taking massive amounts of action over a sustained period of time.

"Anyone can succeed with the ultimate principle of success: small, consistent action over a long period of time. If anyone can master that law through focus, self-discipline and confidence, there isn't anything that's impossible to accomplish."

Check out the other book in the "7 Laws" series today!

amazon.com/author/briancagneey

Made in the USA
San Bernardino, CA
27 April 2017